Ten

Ten

JENNIFER FIRESTONE

BLAZEVOX[BOOKS]
Buffalo, New York

Ten
by Jennifer Firestone
Copyright © 2018
Published by BlazeVOX [books]
All rights reserved. No part of this book may be reproduced
without the publisher's written permission, except for brief
quotations in reviews.

Printed in the United States of America
Interior design and typesetting by Geoffrey Gatza

First Edition
ISBN: 978-1-60964-289-1
Library of Congress Control Number: 2017934580

BlazeVOX [books]
131 Euclid Ave
Kenmore, NY 14217
Editor@blazevox.org

publisher of weird little books

BlazeVOX [books]

blazevox.org

21 20 19 18 17 16 15 14 13 12 01 02 03 04 05 06 07 08 09 10

BlazeVOX

Acknowledgements

Grateful acknowledgment to *Bone Bouquet*, *Chicago Quarterly Review*, *e-ratio*, *The Original Van Gogh's Ear Anthology*, *Portland Review*, *Typo*, and *Word For/Word*, where versions of some of these poems first appeared.

Deepest gratitude to Geoffrey Gatza at BlazeVOX [books] for publishing this project. Special thanks to Laura Sims for her careful reading and insights, and to Kate and Max Greenstreet, my visionary collaborators, who provided the ten, 10-second films that correspond with this book. Also, thanks to the smart and lively group of women who read portions of *Ten* while managing small children and at times enduring an unbearable amount of noise: Amanda Field, Stefania Heim, Katy Lederer, Caitlin McDonnell, Lynn Melnick, Carley Moore, Idra Novey, Laura Sims and Leah Souffrant. Thanks also to Lindsey Hoover, Dana Teen Lomax, Jill Magi, Jonathan Morrill, Sarah Rosenthal, Joanna Sondheim and Leni Zumas for their reading, attention and support of my writing. And most importantly, thanks to my beloved family, Jonathan, Ava, Judah & Iris, who figure largely in these pages, and who help provide the space for me to continue with this work.

Ten

How much better is silence; the coffee cup, the table. How much better to sit by myself like the solitary sea-bird that opens its wings on the stake. Let me sit here for ever with bare things, this coffee cup, this knife, this fork, things in themselves, myself being myself.

—Virginia Woolf, *The Waves*

A world may be affirmed by the turn of a wing out of the corner of my eye.

—Mei-Mei Berssenbrugge, "Pure Immanence"

If I move toward the glass desk
the building is astonishingly white.
I almost wrote "blind."
The sun's effect.
The two leafless trees operate by wind,
look happy.
When one behaves the brain responds, the gesture
absorbed.
Two animals chase through rotten vines,
giddy.

A certain type of light illumines
and yet that word is lost.
It could be a hearse
but it is too short
and sporty.
The door is glue blue.
That's what comes to mind. Illness.
The blue door is at the bottom
of the brown building to mark
an entrance.

It becomes dark, fear of what a day
has held. Some balcony plants live.
Old ones have more character.
They're austere and
stable. Apportioned nature aware
of its limitation. What one has
just is. Let me stay with sight.
The bird dives into a pine. My mind
says, nest. She vanishes
for so long.

The breeze.
The trees
oblige.
Be still.
Appease
my heart
my
nerve
long
gone.

You woke up and his big face says it was worse than he thought but that's okay the operation was a success. But when Jon takes you back to the building stairs and says go backwards like you're a little crab is it the prompt or the pain that's splitting you? You wish all the pain could arrive right now, not in a masochistic wanting way but just a quick jab, 10 seconds. The visceral is sometimes so much a clearer track. 9 years earlier you were being driven by Jon through the Lincoln Tunnel and you were lying across the backseat, windows down, screaming loudly. What you can say is there was a burning, up, up the body. They had given you the meds too late. Isn't that basic, make sure the patient gets her meds before pain kicks in. You cried right before going in. Yes it's knee surgery, but you pleaded, "I have kids!" It was genuine but you also thought maybe your tears accompanied with saying "kids" would get extra attention, like the surgeon would just glance at your sleeping face and do an extra good job with his knives. Jon says the pain afterwards was terrible for him to witness. He said you were like a wild animal and he felt powerless. You like hearing this perspective because it's not all about you. I mean maybe he has the winning memory here because he has the frame of your face, animalish, and the sounds are more located.

He remembers the geography: the tires touching the road and you were just in the backseat. But you don't want the narration of your own pain infringed upon so that the camera swerves for a close-up of Jon's pain. You are a storyteller. You like the arc of narration though you shun it sometimes. Jon says you tell good stories and you argue about ethics. You're a spinner, a fabricator. You go for effect and affect. You get to be what you want in this pivotal pain scene. The female actress who howls and burns, tearing up bits of cheap vinyl seat with her nails.

Tiresome might be precisely it. Lit as a backdrop,
drooping. The setting moves yet I
remain fixed. The setting is orange and yellow.
The setting shifts. I am a tiresome sea.
Surely, sight has value. Say it. Thoughts
quaking. Quietly I shift,
anxiously awaiting the end.
"I am infinity," claims he. Infinitely calm,
he is everything. A he who
claims it.

They ask if I'll put them in the ground,
if I'll put myself in the ground.
If I stare at two buildings I won't go anywhere
but below is what looks like brush,
wiry plants slanting where the sun
ascends. Miraculously all remain
still, though her cry tilts the words
so slightly. The leaning tower
appears; the cry
subsides.

It appears that the light
waxes objects
makes them glow
and the day
though slow
and slipping
is radiance.
Objective correlative
perhaps,
if that works.

"Do not overwrite your environment"
is what I write.
Transform, transcend, transient.
Tranquilly she coats the snow, though the snow
shows no response. Once nature was grasped
at the tip of her fingers though understood now
as temporal, as really, never. My son says "humans"
as in "Are the humans animals? What eats
the humans?" The human writes:
"She is lost."

Playing operation was strange because the man looked like a dumb human. His nose was clownish. It was like of course you could mess up on a body like that. The buzzing noise when you screwed up was humiliating. You fucked up, loser. Jon got the cylindrical pillow and measured the angle so no clots would occur. And then a chapter or two of pain. You're not sure what that means now but you think it was one coat of paint over and over. You find ways to divide the time to wait for the meds. When this album is over. When the smoothie is finished. And then time gallops or is that pain? Artists need to suffer. How does it go? That your art will be better if you suffer. Wow that's privileged. What about all who suffer every day? Would they make good artists? You've had it with the noise. Every iota of household sound feels unbearable as if the rumbling of a wave is comprised of particles of singular rumbles, not cohesive or tremendous which waves are to you. You fear them because you hear death. Construct something to use the time wisely. Write ten lines a day no matter what. Start on your bed with one of those pillow-desks and gradually shift to your regular desk with your leg on top of three pillows. You will be ambitious. This is an artist's residency not some cheaply constructed Brooklyn apartment. Your birds are exotic.

The air is sweet. You will write those lines and do something. You will be able to talk about this. Despite pain and depression you persisted. It's a winning story. People want it. It begins with a long slate of the day and east coast humidity. Your hair rubber-banded and the same black tank. You can't put weight on your foot, so you have to stay. You can't get the mail or go to the pharmacy. You have to stay and you sit deeper in that body that hopefully will hold. And you look out or in, and that's an ocean.

What I sought is what I seek
unable to discern the scenery.
Has the light filtered through
and so the leaves tint
or flood from an early rush?
She moistened the brush and then
gently dabbed the environment.
"Don't be condescending" said
the artisan. A bright bowl bled
to the top corner of space.

Because it flew; its wing tip cloud-light.
The bough embraced its weight and concealed.
The white snagged the sightline
and another.
The peripheral embrace of a gaze
and then
the urgency to write "paper" or "kite."
May I?
Let an object remain
in its fashion.

The bird buys time.
Vine—a line to the bottom.
This furied world.
Word always comes next. Then
back to bird. Absurdly wondering.
To change the smallest
balcony to a designated play spot.
How to provide the right tools? First,
clean. The argument goes
slow. The inside messy.

Quickly
before time transpires.
The writing chokes. Jokingly,
he said "Wanna hear it: say
knock knock."
The performance never happened
because it was not real.
This is it, this is it, this is it.
Foreboding,
merely ridiculous.

After the operation another artist myth clouds. This one about the parents of artists. They must have had someone who cared about art and cared about them thinking and making art. So what do you mean by "art?" Something about one person's art is another person's . . . There must have been at least a great aunt or crazy cousin who provided tutelage. What is your family story? And what about the stories of women and art. Their secret art. Their art nobody knew about or maybe they did and didn't care. Their art that only could be determined via the ones they were actually helping to make art: husbands, friends, students, fill in the blank. And women and babies and art. Well from that overly-conjunctive sentence you witness how terrible that sounds. You had the baby and the bad knee almost as a package deal. Your body looked at you straight and said, "Who's it going to be?" Post-operation you said, well this baby doesn't like me anymore. Yet it wasn't so matter of fact when you said it. You were crying. That the baby called Jon "Mama." You had to stop nursing suddenly. You were doped up on meds. You get it. The narrative changed. Not the way you wanted or planned. The stories kept ricocheting, flying through car windows. The post-op was the "space" that needed designation. A nice outfit. A frame. Ten. It was clean. It could be done. Ten lines a page. If you did it in a day you'd feel okay. That was work. Nobody required post-op patients to do a lot so this would be just fine. What you presented to people would be taken care of. But what about you? You still had to show up.

To be about this.
Resistance bites.
I stretch into limits.
The wall of green sprawls.
Each at its own.
The green holds light
refracting.
Blinded by
a mind's
eye.

Chirping in the near light, the vines straggle.
I saddled the rail, thought about it.
Magnificent wind splash.
Birds ricocheting. Those tiny fleas.
What I can't see moves. The bees.
Laura Ingalls Wilder:
"Then all the little bees in their bright
yellow jackets came swarming out
with their red-hot stings." The page
flung, children frightened.

What's thought of as a flower
is waste
though its crumpled form
remains lovely.
Blocked from their whistles
until decidedly confrontational.
Thoughts congregate
at the wayside.
Flowing tenderly
from A to B.

To want to hold it.
Raging at you though pursuit is futile.
That raging sea, desire.
Three new mouths shot from above
the nest sharpening its beak.
Satiation strung from the building-scape.
The work will wait and work while waiting.
It becomes about death around now.
Oh you.
To affix the loss away from.

The night before an operation you should see a movie. Let your mind roll with waves. You should eat right up until the cut-off. Call a friend and chat like it's a nothing night. But what about after? It's like the operation when you had the baby. But there's more of a script there, so anticipation actually does translate to a new subject. But after just an ordinary operation pain is there. A bridge you cross repeatedly. A whipping flag. A conversation about pain, in pain, can exist periodically, briefly, but cannot persist. Nobody wants that. Even you. So you change subjects. Or go inward and coast. There is marveling at how well you survive. That you're sturdy. And you are, perhaps. So you have Ten to imagine. Ten you are imagining. A title can suggest significance for those who are interested. You are interested. You add a constraint. Besides the bad knee, the meds, you will stare out this one window from your desk. You think: "I always look out this window." But now you will hold that view. Preserve it. One might feel you are being forced. That is true. Or might feel you are being present. Also true. You don't meditate so you're awkward, struggling. You say this is "present practicing" for lack of what it might or might not be. The time divides when the pills are administered. The window is a screen, a painting, a dream. You the artist note-taking, sensing the paradoxical: being fixated and moving full force. The birds are performing, so it seems, for you. They are paired and singular, engaging your sight so you say out loud "Brooklyn holds many birds." There is water running somewhere close by. A squirrel crosses a line and something metal drops. The voices conflict and claim each their note. Dart in and overlap. Where are you? Why not map this. Walk out as far as you can in the water before going under. Set your eyes on the sun. If the bar is low, slip under, slide.

Bones in earth. Early on
discussion shifts. One's back
shifts, earth plates. One day
you will be without me. Harmony
of school songs. "Friends, friends, friends
we will always be."
What is the year
holding? Early on
I awoke to her loud tunes. Soon
we will be in cold weather.

I have 1,000 ways to write "light"
but reiterations descend. A nest of details
presented. I will write away from this,
a glass blue flower wavers, red middle,
translucent. *Away with this.*
Kindness might be the only path.
Blast off. A robot malfunctioned
on the wood floor. "Booooring."
Wordsworth wrote better before
becoming Christian.

The rumbling underneath. She called it
a terrifying noise or terrific noise.
An aquarium encapsulated her lower half
all kinds of sea life swimming.
Activity in the tiniest
rings. To engage is to enter.
One minute particle
set the others off
and then
music.

Stay away stay away.
One from the flock
protests,
is it true? Bellows.
Near his window the young fellow
works, remarkably subtle. To think
I didn't notice. And to whom
am I apparent? Selectively
viewing. And then
suddenly.

You just noticed that "Opera" sits within "Operation."
This is what you do now, such puzzles. Funny enough,
you sing, or can privately, and though this might sound
false, it's actually quite true: you are the opera-singing
type. You don't listen to opera, but you are sure your
voice sounds best at an operatic pitch. The first item for
the day: noticing. The leg pitched up on multiple pillows,
the pressing fear of a clot. And green. A mass of green
congregating beyond your window view. You could write
"lush." Or maybe you meant "bush." The meds are
stupefying but also steadying. So here you go. A day
picked up like a napkin. Hold the green and then what.
There are birds inside of it. Many of them. Birds bobbing
on a wire. This place you evaluate for its green and birdly
view. Of course there are buildings and eyes looking from
them but that's what makes the green sizzle. Compress.
When all else fails you quote others. That's what artists
do. It's not false, really. Kathleen Fraser wrote a series
called "Five letters from one window, San Gimignano,
May 1981." The first one written at 4 p.m. to a "Michael"
ends with "How long is the life of a bee?" You kind of get
it, the essence of asking this question. You imagine you
could find curiosity within your own dull tracks. Perhaps
even write this now. You're only five lines through. The

birds have landed, rested and flown. Who gets to arbitrate what is art and what remains periphery? Who made the head boss "Boss?"

"Buuuhrd." The bird house sits transmitting light.
What a sight the sky. Those are clouds.
A brown vine straggles. Giggle.
But why think progressively. A habit
of the human, you mean "hum." I'm done
with moving fast. At last, alas. Your curls
all atopple. That tree a steeple.
What would one do with names of species?
The science blinks
at the scientist's swagger.

You look like you have a lot to say or is that flutter?
Why not enter the home and eat the seeds?
Resistance to a hole in a wood house.
The white ghost flaps, my mistake,
a moth. Another month
resting. Surely moths dislike holes.
Where's the cardinal. She said "lucky."
Selecting nature—
"They won't come to me!" Shiny objects
illusively inviting.

The swelling. Could be an enormous wave. Well,
close to it. Always in water—so your thoughts.
Farther away than noticed. Well.
Ten seems somewhat bare today.
For what? Wet ropes—sea knots.
Noting the temperature by leaves. The breeze.
Well, inside thickening. She notes
atmospheric dips. And at four someone at
the door,
regulating.

Who was the first and how did they build,
how was street "street." You named us
these names but who was the first?
Curtain askew. You knew I'd be rushing.
Resultant nature. Your features—hard
with shine. "I'm worried
about grades." It becomes academic.
Light was just wet. Now not.
Inching to a storm. Brainstorming,
who are the speedy readers?

The striking fact about your operation is that the doctor had to implant a cadaver's cells into your knee. This, you are told, is experimental. You are also told before the operation that the doctor will somehow manage to keep a stock of these fresh cells on hand when he looks inside. The idea is that the doctor is not sure that he will need them but he will manage it so that the cells are available. You wake up to a throb that really is not a throb as a throb seems more compact. Maybe you are not human but 100% throb. The implant is described to you as a pothole that was just covered up and must be cemented over, hardened. Somehow that is what needs to happen underneath your knee cap. A mysterious world hoping to thrive. At least you have one shred, or cell of what you hope will make a good story. At least there's that. Ten lines felt embarrassingly under-achieving. Like when you're taught the five-sentence paragraph. Ten is a blink. A stretch before workout. The nod when you don't feel like saying hello. What is valid for your ten? Is this one too rushed or filled with pause? Why would you ever choose a number that has been decreed as a perfect score: "She's a ten." "You received 8 out of 10." You know you are prone to give in to these cultural markers. That you want perfection as much as the next. And here you are with your neat block of this or that, swiping one cloud to the side after another. Here you are.

This time availing. Barely showing up.
The sun shines, so be it. Paper strips
flipped, moving towards dissolution.
Gold seeps through.
Equipped to shift—
Egyptian themes so you fancy
so you dream. The red she reads
is bleeding. Light rises,
high rises,
heating.

Until you can't stand it,
stammer.
And when the light drenched or disappeared
what says the subject. Shiver.
Flat palate or modern tint,
she hints at the options.
Choices are chores so she dawdles.
It's best to self-select, ride with pride
and shoot. And the red admirals sweep
a grey horizon.

Suddenly the ivy climbed. We said
no to Ivy as a name. Poisonous. "What did
Ivan sing?" "Ivan working on the railroad."
Your laugh splashes. I flinch.
It's confusing when light appears
as night is almost here. And to think,
we really have no idea what's on
their minds though we find
the expressive exceptionally
fulfilling.

A window
frame
and slicing wings
pressed
translucently.
Where it broke
no mistaking
sound.
Thud replacing
song.

You definitely have to say "operation" because there is something hitting to the bone about it. "Surgery" is all mechanics. "Procedure" is a euphemism that brings up all kinds of questions. But "operation" has a classic, grandiose quality to it. Like "entrée." There is a performance. You are told by your doctor that you will progress in percentages: at first 100% of your foot can't touch the ground. Then 90% of the time you do a heel walk. Then your big toe can join the picture. Yet now you are still in the early stages, your percentages are high, meaning your ability to move, very low. To use the toilet you must fall with the dive of a roller coaster dip. To get into bed it helps to have someone hold your leg like a crane truck that's lifting a heavy object. You watch the person hold it, hold it, until he looks at you for direction. You're flat on your back. When you wash you use a hand sprayer attached to your shower nozzle. You perch on a bench and pretend to clean. You acquire lavender satchels near your bed. The idea is to freshen up, give things a twist. When you've stretched out each menial task as far as they might extend, putty that becomes so thin it's stringy, you look at Ten. There it is, bricks stacking. Its tidiness deceiving. The words rush, then slip.

I insist the strain of sight is effective.
And look the cardinal arrives as conjured.
Dear, these sentences are weighty romantics.
Agreed?
I shook the subject and squeezed its brittle neck.
The black squirrel assumed the antagonist.
The setting is mild and perhaps a little meek.
Sneakily she edges back to the sloshing sea.
The sun glaring her notes
gleefully.

A hump of washed clothes can
never look artistic. I know there
is life, see the leaves wiggle. And
then small particles floating but
they had wings. Seemingly unsure
of how she sets the stage. "Family is
love and help." "Huh?" I'm helping you,
see. Absurdly the bird looks as if
invading. I could very well be
the enemy.

Circuitous sights. When you press
there. Time to write. The sun
streams. Fragile in its
boil. But I want to go–
and that is here. A bright-boiled
fighter I've become. She sang,
"No, I don't know the sex, I just wrote it."
A story sings. The bird, an instrument
strumming,
a hand commanding.

Just let it be
becoming also.
The judge
judiciously
resigned.
Signs of
death-days
coming.
Still
insisting.

The hope is as such—the physical constraints from the operation become full of possibility, promise. In the future you will teach a class called Poetic Constraints. You will use yourself, your knee, as an example. It's only later you realize your students might not want to hear this. The constraints they're fine with. Those are sexy, daring. But your constraint, no thanks. They don't want to picture your knee of all body parts available. Or perhaps they just don't want a body. But there you are conflating body with thinking. Once at a bell hooks lecture she said she purposefully moves her body in a classroom. She said students don't want the body, they want teachers tucked behind desks. Inanimate objects making noise. Deadly classroom silence always preferred over a full-fledged body. Particularly a gesticulating female body. Ten rises. An artist should crave alone time. An artist shouldn't need direction. How come silence is what produces the noise? But it's the book of expectations fluttering its pages. The vacation that awaits urgently and when arriving droops. Your knee, a crystal ball that offers no light. You know the sun is setting when the shade travels in.

Write my mind,
does death follow?
The sense of shallow response.
"Whatever!"
Recycled expressions cycling in.
Random transactions that paved you.
"Were we born when she died?"
And what might that look like?
I shake myself down,
inking a portrait.

There are two and the light douses no longer.
I write "mates." Her eyes hover
above, will she dive below?
Why the onslaught of butterflies and what harbinger
at bay? Symbolic stepping through.
Arising from a stronger place
her face equally presented.
"Resentment will only leave you frail."
The ten haunts but guides,
wings slip through.

Still tense
the sound from blown
air terrifically loud
hear ye, hear ye.
I stretched
my neck
or did I leer?
The interruption–
whips
the horizon.

In a fist her wrist broke words
that's all that time allotted.
"She has more than me" —
that's "a lot."
And with the miraculous surplus
of bees and butterflies
the world seemed full.
Still saying the glass
ain't empty but that's a trap
spinning.

You like when people say "The operative word here is…"
Your listening becomes immediately attuned, a dog's ears
that prick at the first sense of sound. Really you can be
quite simple. Or what you heard on a radio interview
when a journalist was asked "But how were you conned?"
and the journalist responded, "Vanity, pure vanity." You
hear what you want, or try to. While you untie this idea a
burn is creeping, your body's asleep but an alarm sets off.
You'd forgotten your scheduled meds. Pain, a soothsayer
staring you down. Jon is feeling left out or so you think.
You haven't written him in for pages. And if you ask Jon,
you are no angel of a patient. You instruct how he can
obtain crackers and dried fruit. You yell if your door is
not sealed as a vault. Lettuce should be fanned delicately
onto your plate. Notebooks in all sizes surround you,
where ink blurs ideas you're compelled to share. And you
don't want to feel the end of a sheet wrestling with your
toes. What can be controlled, coerced? When you write
Ten all seem to enter: a meow, wind. You bully Ten, abuse
it—try to shape it, make it obey. Too bad the body is a bad
actor. Anxiety a coarse soup.

Stretched to its utmost ends the canvas shimmered
the trees obliged by performing stillness.
The small flea suddenly inside my frame
fled to the hall light.
In light of my subject what shall I
capture?
The flea was actually a house fly and
how is that named?
Meanwhile light adores its reflections,
dressed in a soft hue.

Who are the bad guys raise your hand.
Well understandably you can't acquire assertiveness
just by thinking. The milky sky retreats and she
eats words. However one might be listening
the atmosphere glistens.
"Is that photo of her dying?" "No. she's alive
and smiling." A kind of treaty to attend to
this penning of what's heard. The blank
stare stamps, what's out there
seized.

An elegant sheet of rain exquisite in its glow.
"Where are you?"
"Where do the animals go?"
Nature droops weighted from water and yet more beautiful, "Which outfit is prettier?"
Neon pink and silver lines drown the peeping leaves. Aware and noting material is barely responding.
Aware the end is near.
Not a sheet of rain but shiny pane of glass.

Let us settle tenderly to sleep
the lines blanket
and so thankfully
covered.
Here's to
lack of speed
impediments
tangents
breaking light
for ten slow minutes.

"Ration" also sits within Operation. It's right there though you missed it time and time again. The choke, the limitation. You see Ten could be looked at as the doling of a small dessert. Just enough to arouse the tongue, yank. But you can achieve a lot in Ten. In a sentence love can be made. What you want to say is this window contains a striking amount of bursting flowers. That you see all and each. That voices drift in with the tide. That a bird and an air conditioner. Sun and lights. That vision might erase glass temporarily. Jon opens the door. "A productive day?" He asks this on most days. His way is not monitoring but checking in on you who is anchored. "Productive," that might be the word without nuance, the film scene where the assertive hands grab the heavy curtains in the darkened room and rake them open. Light pours in like a slap. It's difficult to be adaptive. Even further, to see beyond. Your neighbor, Pam, calls you up with a goal in mind: Get you out of the apartment. At this point the doctor says things like "Build up your strength," random fortunes streaming to the sky. You want to know how this looks in the concrete. How you turn the key into the engine to create motion. Pam is at your door. Her voice claps in rhythm, "Let's go." Outside at the top of the steps it's like this: placing the crutch on *the first step and then swinging your body to catch it was like falling towards death. There's no assuredness that everything would be okay. You know somehow you did it. But the "how" is fuzzy. You were hoping you'd use it as a story about courage. But all you see are white squiggly lines. The restaurant she has you hobble to is a block away. A corner spot with a candy red awning. You remember your body there. A black iron chair, your knee propped on another one, which prompts the waiter to engage you. Pam urges you to "Go for it," to order something exciting. You decide on vegetarian tacos as one of the ingredients is huitalacoches. Pam asks what it is but the waiter doesn't know either. The word is a stranger. You don't want to break Pam's heart. You don't want to break. You're not a lunching companion. Later you look up huitalacoches, "Corn smut. A fungus grown on some varieties of corn; a delicacy." It's hard to know what's what. Let it float within the frame.*

Jennifer Firestone is the author of five books of poetry and four chapbooks including *Story* (Ugly Duckling Presse, forthcoming), *Ten* (BlazeVOX [books]), *Gates & Fields* (Belladonna* Collaborative), *Swimming Pool* (DoubleCross Press), *Flashes* (Shearsman Books), *Holiday* (Shearsman Books), *Waves* (Portable Press at Yo-Yo Labs), *from Flashes* and *snapshot* (Sona Books) and *Fanimaly* (Dusie Kollektiv). She co-edited (with Dana Teen Lomax) *Letters to Poets: Conversations about Poetics, Politics and Community* (Saturnalia Books) and is collaborating with Marcella Durand on *Other Influences*, a book about feminist avant-garde poetics. Firestone has work anthologized in *Kindergarde: Avant-Garde Poems, Plays, Songs, & Stories for Children* and *Building is a Process / Light is an Element: essays and excursions for Myung Mi Kim. She won the* 2014 Marsh Hawk Press' Robert Creeley Memorial Prize. Firestone is an Assistant Professor of Literary Studies at the New School's Eugene Lang College and is also Director of the Academic Fellows pedagogy program.

33621229R00043

Made in the USA
Middletown, DE
18 January 2019